Serurubele

poems by
Katleho Kano Shoro

modjaji books

First published by Modjaji Books 2017
PO Box 121, Rondebosch, 7701, Cape Town, South Africa

www.modjajibooks.co.za
info@modjajibooks.co.za

© Katleho Kano Shoro

ISBN: 978-1-928215-28-8

Layout and design by Fire and Lion
Cover artwork by Tammy Griffin and Karen Lilje
Author photograph by Vus'umuzi Phakathi

Contents

In the name of poetry

In the name of poetry
I offer you these words,
translations of thought and
symbols of feeling that fester and ferment within.
I offer you remnants of poets who have taken me to church,
spoke the word
and prayed for my soul as they bore their own.
I offer the time it takes to speak to my heart and
then dare to commit its vulnerabilities to memory.

Ka dithoko
Kea inehela
Mojalefa wa Bakwena le Basia,
Ngwana wa Kapa as well as Jozi.
I offer you my perspectives,
my many mothers' teachings.
I present both hopelessness and moments that excite,
the taxi mgosi that makes me write.
I even offer you these butterflies of mine, if you'll accept the invite.

In the name of poetry
I speak *with* you
in the hope that you find your own words,
offer others parts of yourself by being you,
pray for others in whatever form God chooses for you,
and find God in your language too.
Ka thato ea Modimo le Badimo,
it is in the name of poetry that I've come to you.

Living Libraries

Our libraries move
They have mouths
Dikgeleke speak details in languages complicated to mere theoretical
	linguistic proficiencies
Yet on our skins, masene settle comfortably.

Our libraries move
With analogies alone, Griots run races, solve imbroglios, set new standards
Proverbs bring those who have stepped out of line and been disqualified
Back to the starting line.

Our libraries move
They spread themselves ochre thin
Infiltrating those spaces that knew only of dark and dust
They weave aesthetic means to enlighten us.

Our libraries move
Dunes pace our footsteps and thoughts alike
Streams demand our silence before we answer
Peaks ask us to reflect on who we would like to be hereafter.

Our libraries move
Even in death, Badimo and healers find the means
To help us decipher uncertainties
Narrating lost, convoluted manuscripts through our visions and dreams.

Our libraries must move!
They must hold colloquiums
In skyscrapers, under desert suns, in caves too
Under baobabs and corrugated roofs
Our libraries have work to do.

They must move
Teach notation and words
In languages spoken by people
Of our worlds.

They must move
Even when we are under construction
They must strengthen their content and help us rework the systems
Of categorisation and symbols of our existence.

Our libraries must move
No
Our libraries must live!

Remember me: Cape/Burg

I stood between two grand cities as each of them whispered, 'Remember me.'

Jozi was lean,
her walk packed with ambition,
her hair gelled in a cosmopolitan composition.
She wore a suave scent laced with aspiration
and tied her thick confidence around her waist with extra intention.
I had to catch up to her.
Jozi's pencil skirt matched her high heels coloured in pastel energy.
With every kwai-kwai came a plan,
with every street corner she moulded a wise man.
Jozi walked maboneng;
I had to stand back to catch my breath and adjust my eyesight to her light.
As I watched her stride,
I noticed how her rhythm was inspired by the bassline from Bree Street
        taxi frenzies,
how di-kip-kip reminded her of childhood simplicities,
and how she kept bopping her head to Gandhi Square after-school
        cypher beats.
Jozi finally waited for me,
smiled because she was the daughter of pirates and chiefs
and still knew the perfect spots to feast on lightly salted chicken feet.
For a moment in brief,
she took off her branded shades and I spotted her golden humility.
Jozi, the celebrity, reached out to secretly touch Cape Town's arm,
whispered, 'Remember me',
and carried on walking.

I stood between two grand cities as each of them whispered, 'Remember me.'

Cape Town said it in a light breeze.
His smooth baritone made my frantic heart freeze
as he reminded me to just
breathe.
He maintained his cool pace by letting beach sand filter through his
    crooked toes,
and how he always captured a bottle of perfect Merlot,
not even he knows.
I tried to rush him to catch up to Jozi,
but Cape Town just strolled.
He spoke slow,
telling me how he frequently had lunch with visiting ladybugs on
    mountaintops,
how, from up there, it felt like the Atlantic warmed itself under his feet,
and how fresh air made life easier to eat.
Winds lifted his linen shirt from his fertile chest,
while winter rains made his bare feet wet.
Unphased, Cape Town continued, telling me how he appreciated a
    breyani mess
and cried whenever he thought of Clanwilliam in living context.
Mr Cape Town spoke of ironies like beautiful bergies and short stories
    about long streets.
His Kaapse taal swept between his naked gums as he punctuated in
    Xhosa clicks.
He had time to tell me many things (and still write to Jozi)
but it's the peace he fed me as we wandered through his Garden Route
    that articulated:
'Remember me'

I stood between the two cities and asked them to remember me.

Spit not swallow

Drink up!
Know what bitterness swirls in your mouth.

Spit it out!
We have become too comfortable with swallowing disasters.

Truth watered down

You
poured
through my fingers
carrying my salt, fear and longing
for you. Even as I watched you fall, you
seemed to cling to me. Until
you took
the
leap.
You said
I could hold you, so my
fingers curved their waists, squeezing
the air from between each other. My palms
cupped tightly so you could nestle
in their arc.
Ten dry,
dirty nails pointed
into the air, waiting. But you
slid through, deserting all with a
sneer, intending only
to drip.
You
were never
going to cleanse them,
were you? You never planned to confer
with my dirt or quench me or stay in my palms so I could
drink you through cracked lips, feel you slide down my throat and soak my
shrivelling palate. You were never mine to have or to hold. You did nothing but entice
desiccating finger spines to remind me that I need you. Dear Water, I need you more
desperately than I need the sky from which you are meant to fall. But
as it turns out, this national treasure isn't for all.
Not at all.

Animals of colour

1971
Lavish green park
Sky lined with pink and purple hues
It's almost dark

1971
Grey pigeons no longer allowed to sit on brown 'Whites Only' benches
Policeman, white,
full blue uniform of law and prison doors
had overheard black Oswald
pondering how grey pigeons
broke holy separatist laws
inked in black on white.

Policeman, white
– a little red that black Oswald pondered right –
could not let the holy laws down.
Holy Separatist Ideology:
this is how God intended it to be!

Policeman, white and red
reached out, snatched grey pigeon
choked it
for the watery white and solid brown shit it left on the 'Whites Only' bench.

Pigeon, grey
tossed into the van.
Oswald, black
tossed into the van.
Two animals, grey and black
after curfew
tossed into the van.

Because animals of colour belong in cages.
Right, Officer Valentine?

A response to Oswald Mtshali's poem 'Pigeons at the Oppenheimer Park'

Blasphemy

Bow down and praise me.

I am the religion sold as a delicious dream.
I am the God who led you to slavery via false missionaries.
I am the truth that helped you forget the truth
and now
Badimo ba lona ha le khone ho ba peleta
empa laka lebitso le tswa ka dinko tsa lona tse se para,
dinko tse fapaneng ho bona bale who conveniently inscribed their rights
        to trade you,
as long as the name of God they used.

God.
Ke tla re Modimo ke mang when I know the word God?
Nita sema Mungu ni nani when I know the word God?

God, I wish I knew you true; I wouldn't blaspheme in this bitter tune.
God, I wish I could pray and believe the 'Our Father' made ghetto dreams
        come true.
My granddaddies bartered everything they had in exchange for You,
the same god who had them swinging to the blues and singing
        'Amazing Grace'
how sweet the sound of freedom they will never taste.
I, too, proudly verbalise Oxford's definitions of freedom
but when it comes to enunciating its meaning, ho peleta is a mother!
So keep your notions of freedom and leave us space to be our kind of free.
Keep your stories of a lightly tanned Jesus
and acknowledge my ancestry even in that history.
We are in the midst of calling on names from our own black ancestries

As a past-native, I messed up!
I failed to see that the Holy Bible was their trick and their treat.
I failed to inhale the lines in between that covered up sexism, slavery and
      rights to superiority.
Even as a past-native woman I longed to be a Virgin Mary,
forgetting to question whether I'd still be leader of that story if Joseph
      could have babies.
So as a woman I took the blame:
I am a descendant of an Eve who twisted an Adam's arm
to put her apple between his teeth.
But I dare not speak of the slippery, sly angel serpent
who snuck up behind an Eve to help her discover her sexuality;
even I realise that is blasphemy.

Ndaneta!
I'm tired of living in the hope that my death will one day bring
      significance to my life.
Ek is 'n bietjie gatvol of being pumped full of daai man se conspiracies
      about religion bettering my life.
Too many people die IN THE NAME OF JESUS. AMEN!
Amen?

Too many believers' intestines are exploded and left to dry;
the fruits of holy genocides.
Too many worshippers die,
believing that detonating their insides
will free another's mind.
I am tired of seeing babies turned into refugees,
needing to run and hide in the hills
because they're being killed
whether or not they're ready to believe in anything.

Before you hate me because I'm Christian,
terrorise me because I'm Muslim,
doubt me because I'm pagan
or fear me because voodoo is my religion,
can you look at me as if I were human?

Spit fire!

Spit fire!
Breathe out smoke.
Your brain is going up in flames
as you skate through new ideas
leaving the old ones covered in burnt coal.

Spit fire!
Then pull air in.
Hold your breath,
let the oxygen – fresh –
find every hidden fuse,
let those thoughts grow bigger, fume better.
Get your lungs and blood used to this fiery side of you.

Spit fire!
Breathe out smoke.
Skating Dragon, kick, push and coast.
And when you're in the air,
see the dry ramps and winter grass
staring up into your face
Then,
Spit fire!
And watch the world around you ignite in your flame.

Lekker juicy childish dreams

Sometimes adults forget that we matter.
They tell us to dream as long as our dreams aren't too big and foolish.
They tell us to sing as long as we don't make a geraas with our songs.
They teach us to smile as long as our bright, childish teeth don't distract
        them from being serious.
And when we play our songs and skip through juicy dreams,
they remind us to wipe off our unexplained happiness along with the mud
        on our feet.

Other times, adults forget that when we were too small to even speak,
they told us secrets about how amazing love is
and how we can be anything we want to be as long as we believe.
But as we grow and ask questions, we're told that the future is ours
and so only in the future can we ever speak.
Even when we dream with our big, fat, healthy hearts,
they tell us to remember that it's all just make-believe.

I don't want to be an adult if it means I forget how to sing and dream and
        be happy.
If that's how it's supposed to be,
I want to have the body of a grown-up and the soul of a baby.
I want to make up songs with other big babies who sing and believe just
        like me.
And then, when we become Oupas and Oumas,
I want us to be able tell our grandchildren that the sky is NOT the limit
because people have already landed on the moon!

Right now, as a child,
I want adults to remember that we children matter too.
Not only on June 16 but all the sunny mornings that God wakes us up to.
If our Creator made us strong enough to be kings and queens in heaven,
then we must have enough gold in our souls to be glorious on earth too.
I just want to be allowed to believe in the impossible, lekker dreams
my holy brain was created to produce.

But since adults sometimes forget,
it's up to us to remember that our dreams echo God's tune.
Our laughter and songs are the kinds God sings along to.
We children have to believe that we don't only matter in our dreams.
Our Creator made us alive today and vandag is where our value should be.

Deliciously beautiful

You're deliciously beautiful.
Your heart must be in the shape of a pit-less peach
because all I ever want to do is dip you easy in my mind's cream,
take petite bites out of you ... slowly
so I can savour even the scent of your being.

You imbue my skin with your piquancy,
hide hints of self-rising in it
plant pieces of your peach within my dark chocolate.
You are swirls of decadence
teaching my tongue your essence.

Your delicious is in abundance.
It overflows like sap from watermelon calabashes
          and never touches the ground
because I would dive, fall, scrape both knees, just to get a taste of thee.
Still, your red-bush leaves heal me.
You nourish me ... beautifully.

S'ponono

In warm wafts
you explain to me
how you're able to hold the sun in your right hand
and beckon the sea to your feet
yet the two never realise that
even before picturesque sunsets
they meet in *your beauty*.

Translations

Tell me love in your language;
I'll whisper you a smile in mine.
Hold my hand in two Latin syllables;
I'll impress upon you my state of mind.

I remember you …
You're that guy who said je t'aime ka Sesotho,
had your interpreter translate your English accent with Arabic syntax
and said you fell in love with the olive green you saw in brown skin.

Yes, I remember you …
Distinctly.
When I asked you of your politics
you ran my fingers across your thighs
so I could feel how Greek mythologies are etched with Nubian deities

Silently, you explained to me
how the Shona were engulfed in the arms of the Beti
when they fell in love with the Chinese.
And when you arb'ly mentioned how
the Swati sailed ships built in Aboriginal castles of literature,
I enjoyed you utterly.

So,
here's a thank you kiss
blown in the language of appreciation.
I hope you can translate it.

Sesotho sa ka will not be written in italics

Sesotho sa ka will not be written in italics.
Next to English, Sesotho sa ka, too,
will have her back up straight
because I have decided to make it
a back-up-straight kind of poem.

Sesotho sa ka will not be written in italics.
Not unless italics is the theme of the poem
or that exact line needs to
slant so that when I recite it I know to lean back and emphasise hore ...

Sesotho sa ka will not be written in italics.

Pen

I begged her to bleed
to make her point incisively,
to leave pieces of her victory,
to say anything,
(even if it was just letting out her mo(u)rning breath;
       it didn't have to be sweet).

I had to slit her wrists for her; I wasn't sure she was alive
but I couldn't imagine where she found the time to die.
I needed only a tear:
not much,
just enough to stain … enough pain to pry the seal of her silence.

But she refused.
Refused to be beaten into talking,
charmed into smiling,
taught into feeling.
She wouldn't hear of life.

The poet and her habit

The poet overdosed,
swallowed words until she spat out verbs,
and gagged on adjectives that stopped on the tip of her tongue.
The poet drank local intelligence,
the kind that comes in six-packs and crates and altogether amounts to
        99% of intoxicating phrases
(the other 1% – clichés that come with living on 'the stuff').
Drunk, she urinated formal synonyms that smelt of colloquial diction.
The poet inhaled idioms
and smoking metaphors filled the air.
She stuck sharp sarcasm into her arm,
got high
snorting disordered syntax
through a punctuated note of grammar.
This morning she woke up hungover
from creating antonyms out of euphemisms.
Now look at her,
trying to concoct colours from simile and tautology.
The poet,
the word junkie,
expanded the boundaries of apostrophes
and after taking shots of verse with her,
she's convinced everybody that they too possess creativity.

Absent performer

It had been a while
since I meant the words I'd written
with intention and feeling
and once-upon-a-time meaning.
I'd memorised my lines so finely
I no longer had to think;
they slid out,
following the smooth, muddy path
their predecessors left behind from the trudge of trying to remember
The text had stained memory.
No rehearsing:
the sentiments that once came with reciting
could be performed
with tone,
on-call dramatic pausing
and timed smiling.
Gestures established in the first few tries of muttering lines
stuck.

As usual, I would mark my territory,
employing the identity of the shy girl
who finds her confidence when she grasps the mic
and grabs her voice from the back of her consciousness.
I anticipated the audience's clap.

But just as I got on stage and started the unholy ritual of
reciting rehearsed tunes and talking out a love song,
I spotted a couple kissing in the dark little gontjie,
unfazed by my staged presence,
kissing as if I was their audience.
Those two sucking face at the back, back, back, back
made me feel my words again, for the first time.
They made me remember what I owed my audience:
my presence.

A Poem's Home

Not every mic, stage
ear, page
or tone
is suited for that poem.

Don't discard it
at first disregard.
Together, roam,
find its home

Men of Fire

Black men.
The kind uncomfortable with their dark and night,
gathered around a fire
they'd used their own lives to ignite.

These men knew everything about fire:
They spoke with black labels lacing their breath
spirits warming their chests
it is fire they would ingest,
whenever their paraffin-lit homes exploded,
fuelled by their black-man fire
their black-man stress.
Homes overheating
kids choking
whenever these fathers of fire
were inside.

For a long time
their mighty black bodies were mere containers of fire.
Routinely, they swallowed blazing disasters
sat fuming, having fiery arguments about who was better –
amaZulu okanye amaXhosa?

Of these fiery confrontations they never grew tired;
instead, these welded them together.

Collectively, tribally,
as they shared their stories of disaster-eating
as they nurtured their anger about everything
their collective fire kept growing.

In unison, they practiced.
They went from coughing smoke to spitting balls of flame.
Black dragons,
it was with fire they secretly played
until they swallowed the blaze again.

This was not enough:
they needed witnesses
needed the world to know they had found work
that they were hard at work.

Feeling like they would burn out
if they didn't create something of brilliance
they created a Burning Man
who was foreign to their fire
so he stood no chance.

Men of fire,
black men who show other black men flames.
What does sizzling skin look like?
To you, does charcoal and their dark tone look the same?
What about the smoke?
Ha mosi o siya mollo … mmele
do you have to cover your nose?
How much petrol does a human body need?
How much of your flame did Ernesto Nhamuave need?

A young debriefing for Sankara

Dear Thomas, Mr Sankara
our visionary martyr
we resurrect your cotton-clad spirit
We, the children of women and workers
whom you once let bloom in it.

The old men who knew how to dye and weave
died and were weaved into a typical African story,
the one where the IMF dictates
the Faso Fani factory's suicide.
At least it was nothing like Namibia's hushed genocide.

Ntate Sankara
Black is still poor
women are still war pawns
and our parents forgot to build black industries
– although we have our Wi-Fi eyes on Kagame.

Upright Man
now, *we're* trying,
quitting nine-to-fives in pursuit of collective creativity
and our colonial education is burning.
It is we who are building and burning!

Upright men

Upright men,
spines
reaching for
the sky,
pride stretching
to be
legacies for boys
whose
curved spines will
need YOU
to love UPRIGHT.
Keep your
posture, walk with it.
What seems
back-breaking in your
youth, will be
the backbone for youth
who come through
you. Prevent poor posturing. Don't
back out. If this is war, then our nation
needs men with your
stature to
win.

Spade

There are stories and aches you've buried in bottomless silence.
The daughter in me believes you are protecting her from the hearing.
The you in me decides it's your own sanity you're preserving.
If, on any quiet evening, you need to unearth them,
the you in me can help carry them in and out of mourning without
      being seen.

Love Poem to Papa I

I used to speak of your existence
in whispers
because in my circle of blackness
fatherly presence is deafening enough
without calling your virtues
by name.

Love Poem to Papa II

Mokwena,
letsatsi le le leng
ke tla ho roka.

Daughter notes

Jazz and soul soothe me and make me feel grown.
I think this means you soothe my soul and jazz up my growth.
I think I mean you are music.

It's not over until the fat lady sings

It's not over until the fat lady sings.

The day our hearts stopped holding hands
I was on the lookout for coco de mer hips
and marshmallow cheeks
bound to vibrate with the moving of her Vienna lips.
Through my glaze of tears
I made sure my sight had enough leverage to scout out the cookie monster,
who was about to confirm that I'd lost my chocolate chip.
The day our hearts' hands broke it off
I thought our heart-shaped rusk was about to be beaten into crumbs or a
       death even worse
– being dipped in her sweet tea or eaten later from the bottom of her purse.

But apparently, we have to wait until the fat lady sings.

So with every step that my jelly-knees knocked away from you
I kept guessing her tune.
I imagined she'd sing something high-pitched;
the kind of note that would dig a ditch into a keyboard
and orchestrate the conductor
or inspire itself to soar even higher
until even heaven's skies cried
as the glory of sunshine was crucified,
blackened by her pitch,
yet the grey clouds could only be parted by her voice's lightning!
But that was in my mind.
So I carried on with my carrot-fed eyes
in the dark of my night because …

It's not over 'til the fat lady sings.

And there
my pumpkin fears reappeared
as I saw this mother of obesity struggling to walk,
her vocal cords trembling directly at me.
I stood as if ice had frozen my body
but allowed my mind to brew in a ginger of paranoia
only later to get drunk on thoughts of being alone.

Dear Miss Cholesterol came closer.
Her voice was as beautiful as I hadn't imagined it to be.
It was the smearing of butter on a hot toasted piece;
it was the smell of coffee roasted in a blend sure to rouse me.
I hated it.
but that tune was like a serving of fresh berries drizzled with honey.

As I was about to gracefully accept that dear Fat Lady had sung
and our end had just begun
she stood still,
only touching my left baby finger,
and it was then that I figured ...
Fat Lady wasn't singing!
Her place was to hum to the songs of that skinny man
who had disappeared into the shadow of her hips
as they walked the streets.

So the question is:
is it not over because Fat Lady didn't sing,
or is it over because she's been married to this skinny man for so long?
Maybe in their union they became *one*,
so he sings and she hums
and that is their song.
Has it been over all along?
Or am I to wait for Fat Lady to break into her solo song?

How do we mourn friendships?

We were never taught how to lose friends,
mourn them,
expect them to break our hearts
or live with the guilt of disappointing them.

No 'Best-Friend-Lost Anonymous'
no articles on 'How to Spot the Warning Signs of a Waning Friendship',
not even tips from the elderly on how to let go.

Where do we go to raise angry, sad fists
and formulate struggle songs
that help us protest
the ending?

What are the steps?
1. Write a letter
2. break up over your favourite bottle of wine
3. cry … alone?

Or maybe:
1. Indulge in the flavour of ice-cream she found vile
2. binge-watch a TV series you never shared
3. find a faux-best-friend shoulder to drain your tears on?

How does your personal dictionary divorce itself from the dialects you
        adopted together,
from the mantras you chanted in unison,
from mottos you coined?

What about the secrets and memories?
Under which best-friend carpet do you have them swept?
Who helps you dig the graves to keep them buried?

How do you heal away from that person who used to help you heal?

Funeral Sounds

Funerals sound like wailing
hearts throbbing, aching
ripping, letting pain in
and allowing it to drip, flow and pour
out of corners of eyes and every tearing pore.

Funerals sound like Sesotho
like accents that travelled from Lesotho
condolences spoken in presence as a show of botho.
They sound like chu-chu-chugging trains, delayed planes
and quiet homes suddenly bursting with dialects from Bloemfontein.

Funerals sound like dithoko. Mouthfuls.
Praise poems whispered to restless bulls.
They sound like the sacrifice's final bellow and the breath it pulls
before exhaling its spirit into the arms of the deceased
personally reciting her through her own ancestry.

Funerals of Bakwena sound like rain
like thunder echoing the survivors' pain
drops of blood and water swirling soil into fane.
Funerals sound like droplets colliding and colluding with tears
the relief of strengthened ancestry clashing with our mortal fears.

Funerals sound like triangles, drums le diphala
'Ndikhokhele' hummed to antagonise the obituary reader.
Difla. High-octane 'koloi ya Eliya!'
They sound like singing your grandmother's favourite hymn
your voice pleading with her keeper to just 'Let. Her. In!'

I quite prefer the funeral sound
to the days after, when you're mourning-bound
Mourning sounds too much like quietening,
like loneliness persisting,
things unsaid, time unticked and life missing.

For Mme Mmaseliane Mpho Elizabeth Ngatane

Unpunctuated ending

He turned
full stops into flowers.
How was I to punctuate our
ending? We went
on …

We are skins

We are skins that know salt.
We turn ourselves inside out,
sweat, heal wounds,
create adornments and warm bodies.

We are skins that know life.
We could speak psalms about the sun's journey
from the mouth of the mountain to
the offing of the sea.
We harbour fly eggs and hopeful futures simultaneously.

We are skins that know stories, tears,
life, death ... years.
We are the skins of those
who bellow to Badimo to let you in.

Ode to Badimo le Baholo

We believe these are simply *our* revelations,
that *we* found the light through complete darkness.

Really,
there have been people in our corner
from the days we wore nappies.
People who began the process,
hoping these would be our revelations, our revolutions.
They taught themselves the art of electricians:
made the bulbs
learnt how to uncross wires
open circuits
and even stock up on units
for our light-bulb moments.
There are also those who fed us carrots
so we could navigate switches in the dark ...

We think these are simply our revelations.
But it took many to turn the lights on.
There will be many keeping the lights on.

Acknowledgements

Firstly, thank you to Modjaji Books for this opportunity. Colleen Higgs you have treated my work – and poetry – with integrity from the beginning and I cherish this warm space into which you have welcomed me. Lauren Smith, dear editor, I am grateful for how you have patiently and respectfully worked and negotiated with me throughout this invaluable process. Thank you to Professor Nyamnjoh for planting the publishing seed and being more than a lecturer and supervisor: you are an inspiration, a mentor and my (academic) father. To my parents, Pulane and Motale Shoro, kea leboha for your endless support and encouragement in everything. Mama, thank you for editing Sesotho sa ka (it'll get there). A huge thank you to my family in general and Malome Malefetsane Ngatane and Mama Yvonne Kumalo in particular, for believing in my poetic abilities before you could even be sure I had any. Mr Welsh, you remembering the line 'I'm fabulous' encouraged me to continue writing and performing from high school.

Poetry Delight and Current State of Poetry (CSP) family: some of my best writing (yet) has come from you inspiring and pushing me to be a more mindful yet adventurous poet. To my friends: I am thankful for all of you! Tshepiso Mahlafuna, you got me started. Khahliso Serei (and Mama Bathabile Serei) you were cheering me on at the beginning. Tiffany Mugo, Siphumeze Khundayi and Nicola Lazenby: you never let me stop (and thanks for the editing). Bulumko 'Jelly Bean' Nyamezele, you're a constant reminder of artistic brilliance and humility – thank you for your consistent support. Dejavu Tafari (aka Vuyokazi Ngemntu), when I needed an extra set of poetic eyes, you edited with honesty and care. Enkosi kakhulu!

Badimo le Modimo: Ke lebohela every muse and stage created, words in abundance, my life and the ability to write. I believe it is through and within muses and wonders like butterflies, experience, histories, people and that which we feel that sacredness exists and poetries are illuminated.

KATLEHO KANO SHORO is a published performance poet and African scholar who holds a Masters' degree in Social Anthropology. She has performed in South Africa, Swaziland and London as well as participated and facilitated in the South African literary festivals: Naked Word Festival, Open Book Festival and  Franschhoek Literature Festival. Katleho Kano is the co-editor of *The Spoken Word Project: Stories Travelling through Africa* (2015) and her poetry has been published in journals internationally. Her work in the arts extends to research, facilitating workshops and managing projects particularly in African film and literature.

Printed in the United States
By Bookmasters